Paul's Prayers

**How to Pray
Effective Prayers...**

...and Get Your Prayers
Answered!

By
VL Wilson

**The effectual, fervent prayer
of a righteous man availeth much.**

Paul knew how to pray to get answers.
He prayed the kind of faith-filled prayers that bring results.
Every word that Paul spoke was taught to him by God's Spirit,
not by human wisdom...
And the same Spirit helps us today.

**The purpose of this booklet is to teach YOU how to pray
those Paul kind of prayers – prayers that get results
and change circumstances.**

My prayer for you is that your trust, assured reliance,
and confident hope shall be fixed in Jesus,
and that you will get your prayers answered.

Copyright © 2005 by VL Wilson

Paul's Prayers: How to Pray Effective Prayers and Get Your Prayers Answered
by VL Wilson

Printed in the United States of America

ISBN 1-59781-251-X

All rights reserved solely by the author. The author guarantees all contents are original and do not infringe upon the legal rights of any other person or work. No part of this book may be reproduced in any form without the permission of the author. The views expressed in this book are not necessarily those of the publisher.

Unless otherwise indicated, Bible quotations are taken from the Contemporary English Version. Copyright © 1991, 1992, 1995 by the American Bible Society.

www.xulonpress.com

Paul's Prayers
How to Pray Effective Prayers and get your Prayers Answered!

Dedicated to :

**A'Lexa Hawkins,
my spiritual advisor,
prayer partner, and equal.**

With Appreciation for:

- ♥ Al and Hattie Hollingsworth who gave me the Spiritual "kick" to put feet to the vision.

- ♥ James the Second and Louis the Third, who freely and with great patience lent their expertise to the project.

- ♥ My many encouragers and supporters -- you know who you are.

Paul's Prayers

How to Pray Effective Prayers and get your Prayers Answered!

TABLE OF CONTENTS

Purpose: Why Should I Read This?	Page 1
How Do I Know What God's Will Is?	Page 3
Why Pray The Word	Page 4
How Can I Get The Faith to Believe That My Prayers Will Be Answered?	Page 5
Prayer Vs. Confessions: What's the Difference?	Page 6
Ok, I'm Ready. How Do I Begin Praying?	Page 8
Sample Prayers	Page 11
Praying Better Prayers through Personalization	Page 14
What Are Selfish Prayers and How Do I Avoid Them?	Page 15
How Do I Establish a Regular Regime?	Page 16
Notes on Negotiating the book	Page 17

Paul's Prayers By Book

Romans	Page 19
1 Corinthians	Page 23
2 Corinthians	Page 26
Galatians	Page 29
Ephesians	Page 31
Philippians	Page 35
Colossians	Page 39
1 Thessalonians	Page 42
2 Thessalonians	Page 44
1 Timothy	Page 46
2 Timothy	Page 50
Titus	Page 52
Philemon	Page 53

Topical Index Of Prayers ....Page 54

Paul's Prayers
How to Pray Effective Prayers and get your Prayers Answered!

Dear Reader,

I used to be one of those people who would pray haphazardly, sometimes getting my prayers answered and sometimes not – but it was a crap shoot, the luck of the draw. Though I loved God dearly and wouldn't have admitted it aloud for anything, I felt like I could not depend upon Him to be there for me when it came to prayer.

I knew the fault lay in me, but that didn't lessen my frustration. Why did some people get their prayers answered – seemingly effortlessly – and I couldn't? My heart knew God didn't play favorites. So, what was the problem?

After much soul-searching and many sleepless nights, **I discovered the secret of answered prayer**. I became like one of those people I used to be jealous of. People began to ask me to pray for them because they could see the changes in my life and in the life of my loved ones. I grew confident to pray -- and expect an answer -- not only for myself, but for others.

The secret? It's in knowing how to pray the Word. I began to study Paul – who always received supernatural intervention and answers to his prayers. I paid close attention to Paul's prayers – what did he pray, how did he pray it? When did he pray? And I began to do likewise. The assurance that he had rubbed off on me. **As I read Paul's prayers and meditated on his confessions, my faith expanded.** My confidence that God heard my cries -- that my prayers were in line with His, and that they'd be answered-- grew.

Some of you, are saying…"that's just it, I don't' know what Words to pray." Or "I don't know God's will for my particular problem." Or "I don't have the faith you have." Well neither did I at first, but I've researched and written down all of Paul's prayers and many of his confessions for you to meditate on at your leisure. **You can do the same thing for it is capsulated in this book.** I've also included answers to such questions as:

How do I know what God's will is?
How do I pray the Word?
How can I get the faith to believe that my prayers will be answered?
How do I begin?
What is the difference between an prayer and a confession?
How do I establish a prayer regime?

Read this book with the mindset that things are going to change, and I guarantee your prayer life will be transformed. **Practice what is being taught within these pages.** Learn how to pray those Paul kind of prayers -- prayers that get results and change the circumstances of your life.

--VL Wilson

Paul's Prayers
How to Pray Effective Prayers and get your Prayers Answered!

Purpose: Why should I read this?

This booklet is to help believers (those who confess and profess Jesus Christ as their Lord and Savior) become better, more effective pray-ers. It will show you how to pray successfully, so that you can *see* the answers to your prayers. Prayer results will become the norm in your life instead of an abnormality. You will come to trust God to hear your cries, and to know that He responds speedily. Through reading this booklet and praying its prayers, you will be assured of God's will and that you are praying His will. For, if we pray according to God's will, He hears us...and if we know He hears us, then we can be assured that our prayers are answered. This is a fact!

Once your prayers reach God's ears, the answer comes. Most of us doubt that God hears us. Past experience tells us that God doesn't answer prayers. Our prayers were not effective. This will change as you read through this booklet. The truth is that God desires to deliver you out of your circumstances and to bring light into your darkness: *"In my distress, I called upon the Lord and cried to my God. He <u>heard</u> my voice and my cry came before Him into His very ears...He reached down from on high; He took me, and drew me out of many waters. The Lord is my rock; my fortress; and my deliverer"* [Ps 18:5,6, paraphrased]

Paul's Prayers
How to Pray Effective Prayers and get your Prayers Answered!

Paul knew how to pray to get answers. He prayed the kind of faith filled prayers that bring results. Every Word that Paul spoke was taught to him by God's Spirit, not by human wisdom… And the s*ame* Spirit <u>helps us</u> <u>today</u>. **The purpose of this booklet is to teach you how to pray those Paul kind of prayers – prayers that get results and change circumstances**.

My prayer for you is that you will open your heart to the revelation on prayer that God has waiting for you and that your prayer life will be revolutionized. I pray that your trust, assured reliance, and confident hope shall be fixed in Jesus…so that you will be free from doubt and unbelief. I pray that as you read Paul's Prayers, your faith will be stimulated and your confidence (in God's faithfulness) will grow. The Holy Spirit will speak to you and guide your steps as you learn how to pray the effectual, fervent prayers of the righteous.

Paul's Prayers

How to Pray Effective Prayers and get your Prayers Answered!

How do I know what God's will is?

Most of us know that God is the Lord Almighty, and that He can do anything, but we're _not_ sure if He WILL do something specific for us: "I have a need. Is God willing to answer my prayer?" The real question then becomes: What is God's will? How do I know what God's will is? The Answer: *God's Word is His will.* When you pray His Word, you are praying His will. The prayer command that God's will be done and God's Kingdom come is a powerful one that breeds change in circumstances. You are praying for God's abundance, deliverance, healing, etc. to come to you. He has stated that His will for you is for good – that He has plans for your future, for a hope that will not be cut off. God's will be done. God's Kingdom come into your life.

Enemies bow and scatter when God's voice thunders. When does His voice thunder? When His Word is being spoken by you, a believer. The earth trembles, angels are dispersed, and the answer to your prayer is dispatched. Believe it. Paul recorded many prayers and wrote many prayer confessions throughout the New Testament. I have written these down for you to copy and recite. God's Word is powerful and alive. His Word creates, and it will create and change the circumstances of your life as you begin praying and expecting His Word to produce and work in you. Read through Paul's prayers, and pray them for yourself. Bring life into your life. Jesus desires it: *"I have come to bring you life and that more abundantly."* [Jn 10:10, paraphrased]

Paul's Prayers

How to Pray Effective Prayers and get your Prayers Answered!

Why pray the Word?

God's Word is constant; it doesn't change. When you pray it, it works 24/7, whether you feel like its working or not. That's comforting because the weight of getting your prayers answered doesn't fall on you. The prayed Word works on its own. It does the work. You don't! The farmer casts seed upon the soil; and he goes to bed at night and gets up by day, and the seed sprouts and grows--how, even he himself does not know.

Similarly, your prayer is seeded and the answer grown. The process of getting results does not change because of your feelings. When you are down, distressed, or depressed, the Word will still work. It changes not. Thus, getting disciplined enough to allow the Word to *pass your lips* will brings victory to you and your circumstances. Pray Paul's prayers *daily*.

His Word is a lamp for your feet, bringing light (understanding, deliverances) to your situations. And because God's Word is a two-edged sword, while it is out there effecting change in your circumstances, it is also effecting change in you! <u>Through the Word, given by Paul, my heart became assured that God is constantly working</u> in me to will and to do according to His good pleasure. I came to believe in God's goodness and willingness to answer my prayers. I came to believe that praying God's Word is not futile or useless, but effective. Believe it. He's working through you also – causing you to want (will) to do what He wants <u>and</u> causing you to actually be able to do it. This is the heart cry of most of God's children. We *want* to please Him. By praying the Word, we can.

Paul's Prayers

How to Pray Effective Prayers and get your Prayers Answered!

Additionally, God's Word does <u>not</u> return void (empty), but it accomplishes what it was intended to do. That's why you have to be specific in your prayer. Isolate and identify what it is you really are asking God to accomplish in your prayer -- because the Word will achieve its intent. When you study Paul's payers, you'll note that he included his intent -- his reason or purpose for praying in most of his prayers: "We always pray that God will show you everything He wants you to do and that you may have all the wisdom and understanding that His Spirit gives. [Now he includes the purpose / intent] *Then you will live a life that honors the Lord, and you will always please Him by doing good deeds.*" [Col 1:9, 10] This prayer will not reach God's ear and fall flat. When you pray this prayer, it is God' Word / will being prayed by you, and through you – it will be accomplished.

How can I get the faith to believe that my prayers will be answered?

Most of us know intuitively that without faith it is impossible to please God. It is also impossible to get our prayers answered. But, what's the solution? How can those with small, weak faith get the faith to believe? Simple. Faith comes by hearing and hearing by the Word of God. Every time you pray the Word you are building up your faith. It is nothing that you <u>see</u> or feel. Your faith is being built up night and day; you just don't know how. What you *can* know is that it is true. God is faithful to answer His Word – God's <u>Word</u> is what doesn't return void. God's Word is what brings about miracles and effects change. Whether you pray from Paul's Prayers, pray a confession or directly from the Word– the Word will be prayed and success is assured.

Paul's Prayers
How to Pray Effective Prayers and get your Prayers Answered!

As you pray God's Word <u>regularly</u>, watch your faith in the Word increase. Watch your confidence -- that God hears you and will respond -- solidify. Watch yourself go from "God is good" to "God is great and greatly to be praised" because He has fulfilled such good things in your life as a response to your prayers.

Prayer vs. Confessions: What's the difference?

I stated that I have Paul's prayers and confessions listed for your review. Why? What is the difference between a prayer and confession, and why do we need confessions. Isn't prayer enough?

When Paul's exact Word prayers are written down, those are direct prayers. You are praying exactly what Paul prayed. However, there are times when what Paul is teaching in the Word speaks to you and you can turn what he is saying into a prayer; it isn't a direct prayer, but it is a prayer. These are called Word-based prayer *confessions*. They work the same way as direct prayers because they are still God's will (His Word) being prayed. Example. You read:

...God is the one who began this good work in you, and I am certain that He won't stop before it is complete on the day that Christ Jesus returns. You have a special place in my heart. So it is only natural for me to feel the way I do. All of you have helped me in the work that God has given me, as I defend the good news and tell about it here in jail. ...<u>I pray</u> that your love will keep on growing and that you will truly know and understand how to make the right choices. (Purpose☺ Then you will still be pure and innocent when Christ returns..." [Phil 1:6]

Paul's Prayers

How to Pray Effective Prayers and get your Prayers Answered!

The top part of this scripture can be turned into a prayer of confession; the bottom part is Paul's direct prayer:

Confession: Thank You God for completing the work that you have started in me. No matter what my feelings or past failings, I know (am certain) that you won't stop before it is complete on the day that Christ Jesus returns. In Jesus' name, Amen

You can then pray Paul's direct words as a prayer also:

Prayer: I pray that my love will keep on growing and that I will truly know and understand how to make the right choices. Then I will still be pure and innocent when Christ returns. In Jesus' name, Amen.

Confessions help to build up your faith. They take the actual Word of God and make it personable and believable *to you*. Since faith comes by hearing God's Word, when you speak out God's Word and confess it over yourself, your faith will grow. I have found that **my prayer confessions actually help me to get my direct prayers answered** because they prepare me to receive. After confessing that God loves me and that it is by grace that I am saved and made acceptable to Him-- not by works or anything that I can do, then I rest and relax. I don't have to earn my prayers being answered. I could have sinned, I could feel down, but that wouldn't stop me from being able to go to God for help, since He's already accepted me.

Paul's Prayers

How to Pray Effective Prayers and get your Prayers Answered!

Because of my confessions, I can more boldly go to the throne of God (through prayer) and know that my prayers will be answered. My confidence level is raised that God will do what He has promised <u>for</u> <u>*me*</u>! That's powerful.

OK, I'm ready. How do I begin praying?

Praying is simple. You can take any passage or text from the bible and make it into a prayer simply by rewording it to make it become personal. What do I mean? Let me show you by example. Read the following account of how easy it was to turn the Word into a viable, effective prayer:

I woke up from a nightmare and couldn't get back to sleep for fear of falling back into the dream and from the fear caused by the dream. I thought about turning on the TV or reading to distract myself, but then decided to go to God. I flipped open the bible and read:

I will look to the hills! Where will I find help? It will come from the Lord who created the heavens and the earth. [Ps 121:1]

I said, "God, I'm looking to you for help in taking away the fear from my dream and for helping me get back to sleep. I'm looking to you and not to the TV.

Paul's Prayers

How to Pray Effective Prayers and get your Prayers Answered!

I continued reading: *The Lord is your protector, and he won't go to sleep or let you stumble. The protector of Israel doesn't doze or even get drowsy.* [Ps 121:3]

I said, " Thank You God for protecting me. I can sleep because you won't. You're protecting me even now. I don't have to be scared.

Last, I read: *The Lord will protect you and keep you safe from all dangers. The Lord will protect you now and always wherever you go.* [Ps 121:7,8]

I then said: Once again thank you. You are my protection now and always. I can go back to sleep as you protect me from <u>all</u> dangers – even the fears in my mind. I love you God. Thanks.

Then I got up and wrote this section. I was inspired. Notice how easy it was to change the written Word into a prayer of confession. I wasn't quoting a direct prayer that Paul prayed, but I was using the Words from the scripture to make my prayer. <u>It was simple, direct, and went straight from my lips to Gods ears</u>. He really, really treasures those who are humble – those who depend solely on Him – who go to Him for help. When you go to Him with your problems or concerns, you are showing Him that you choose to depend upon Him. Prayer is going to God for help and expecting Him to respond favorably. For that confidence, He blesses you tremendously in return.

Paul's Prayers

How to Pray Effective Prayers and get your Prayers Answered!

Read on to learn (1) how to use this book to help you to turn the Word into your own prayers and (2) how to take those prayers that Paul prayed himself and personalize them for yourself.

But, what do I do next? How do I <u>use this book</u> to help me get started?

This booklet is set up to display both Paul's prayers and his confessions. You're not sure of what to say? You can begin by praying his prayers aloud, tailoring them to your situation. There are two ways you can begin.

(1) by reading Paul's prayers as they are written in his letters (epistles): This will give you a chance to discover a variety of prayers on a wide range of subjects. These prayers and confessions are taken from Paul's letters and written sequentially (prayers found in Paul's letter to the Romans, to the Corinthians, etc.) This is a good way of browsing through prayers and discovering new and appropriate ones for you.

Or

(2) by choosing Paul's prayers listed by topic: You can look up specific prayers by subject matter (such as guidance, patience, fear, etc.) in the Topical Index at the back of the book. Each topic is followed by a prayer reference that leads you to where the prayer is found in the book. R6 means the 6th prayer in Paul's letter to the Romans.

Paul's Prayers

How to Pray Effective Prayers and get your Prayers Answered!

Whether by book or topic, read each prayer / passage until something "<u>clicks</u>" with you – something will speak to your heart. The passage will stand out or "hit" you in some way to make you take special notice of it. This is a Word for you that will correct or encourage you. These Words are the Words that the Holy Spirit has made alive to you <u>this</u> day. *Give us this day our daily bread.* [Mt 6:11, paraphrased] Take those Words (the one's that meant something to you today) and repeat them as a prayer. Personalize them, mix them with your personality -- but talk to God using those Words as your launching pad. Here's how. (*Take note of the way I use my personality when I change the following passage to a prayer*):

Sample Prayers

Situation. I am having problems with a co–worker or family member. I read the following passage:

If our faith is strong, we should be patient with the Lord's followers whose faith is weak. We should try to please them instead of ourselves. We should think of their good and try to help them by doing what pleases them. Even Christ did not try to please himself. ... God is the one who makes us patient and cheerful. **[note Paul's prayer here]** *I pray that He will help you live at peace with each other as you follow Christ. Then all of you together will praise God the Father of our Lord Jesus Christ.* [Rom 15:1 ff]

Paul's Prayers

How to Pray Effective Prayers and get your Prayers Answered!

After thinking about what was written, I pray:

Father God, help me to please others and not myself, especially _____ who really gets on my nerves. You said **(*Now here is where I pray the Word*)** that You make us patient and cheerful. Help me. I want to have patience with _____ but I don't want to be hurt or used. **(Here you can directly pray what Paul prayed)** I also pray for both _____ and myself that you will help us live at peace with each other. **(Notice the purpose / intent is given? Remember, God's Word accomplishes its purpose. Also more of the direct Word is prayed here.)** Then both of us *together* will praise God the Father of our Lord Jesus Christ. In Jesus' name, Amen.

This is a perfect example of praying God's will / Word through Paul's prayers. Your **tone** is you. You go to God talking to Him like you would talk to your best friend. You're honest and truthful with Him as you change your situation with His Word.

Notice also, that in praying the above prayer, I personalized it. I made it mine. So must you. As you read the Word, you think about what is being said. Then you pray the life-changing Word, trusting God to bring the Word to pass.

Paul's Prayers

How to Pray Effective Prayers and get your Prayers Answered!

Here's another prayer situation:

Situation. You are having financial problems. A bill is due that you do not have enough money to cover. You read in your bible:

God loves a cheerful (prompt to do it) giver. And God is able to make all grace abound to you so that in all things at all times having all that you need, you will abound in every good work and every charitable donation. [2 Cor 9:7]

You think about what you just read, and then pray:

Father God, I lift this bill up to you and thank you for helping me out of this financial bind. Thank You for making all grace abound toward me so that in all things (especially this bill, rent, etc.) I have all that I need. I do not lack. I'm going to stop panicking and trust you. Because of your blessings and favor, I have all that I need and even abound to do more. Thank You that Your Word is true, in Jesus' name. Amen.

Do you see how the prayer is personalized to your particular problem and for you? Did you notice how the Word was incorporated throughout the prayer? Remember it is the Word that changes your situations and circumstances. It is also the Word that brings faith (Faith comes by hearing and hearing by the Word of God [Rom 10:17]). So you are doubly blessed when you pray the Word.

Paul's Prayers
How to Pray Effective Prayers and get your Prayers Answered!

Praying Better Prayers through Personalization

One big change that helps me a lot in personalizing a prayer is to change the verbs to <u>present tense</u>. When God deliver<u>ed</u> someone, I thank Him for deliver<u>ing</u> me (present tense). I thank Him for continuing to perfect that which concerns me (present tense). <u>In the above prayer, I thank Him for making all grace abound toward me (right now, present tense).</u>

You can also make Paul's prayers yours by changing the pronouns. Change the "you" to "I" and the "they" to "us" Instead of a general, faceless "you," I make the prayer's blessing pertain to ME. **You** are now praying the prayer. Make it yours. The resulting change in your circumstances certainly will be!

My desire for you is that you learn to pray God's Word/will over a circumstance or situation and have immediate peace, knowing that God has your back and does, indeed, answer your prayers. Bowing your knee to God's Word – submitting to pray His Word in your life is a huge step in getting there.

Just today I told God how I really didn't want a certain person to have a happy life, BUT that it wasn't my will, but yours that I agreed needed to be done. So I prayed a blessing for that person. The Word went forth. His will is being done in that person's life and in my circumstance, and I am at peace. That is what I want for you. Pray God's Word over you and yours – even when you don't want to. The result will be worth it.

Paul's Prayers

How to Pray Effective Prayers and get your Prayers Answered!

What are Selfish Prayers and How do I avoid them?

Do not be selfish in your prayers. Selfish prayers are prayers you pray only for yourself; include others in your prayer time. God's purpose and design is to have us comfort others with the same comfort that we ourselves receive from Him. Therefore, we should focus not only on ourselves, but on others as well. Let's enlarge our tents. There are other people needing the same help and comfort that you receive from the Word. Give it to them in prayer.

Jesus prayed, *"Father, the time has come for You to bring glory to Your Son...My followers belong to You and I am praying for them...Keep them safe by the power of the name You have given Me. (Purpose) Then they will be one with each other, just as You and I are one...* ***I am not praying just for these followers, I am also praying for everyone else who will have faith because of what My followers will say about Me...*** [Jn 17:1, 15-20]

Jesus included <u>us</u> in His prayers by a single line. You can include others with a few words also. The benefit is astounding. We are still reaping and being protected by God because Jesus wasn't selfish in His prayers. Let's be unselfish also.

Paul's Prayers

How to Pray Effective Prayers and get your Prayers Answered!

I almost never pray just for myself anymore. I will pray, "God, help me and the other people in my extended family who are feeling like me right now." It is soooo easy to change a selfish prayer into a generous one and affect the lives of many. All I did was include their names in the prayer. One prayer does double time. Sometimes I pray for me and then add on the others. God has enough power to help us all. We won't use it up if we include others in our prayers. Jesus, our greatest example, did it.

How do I establish a regular regime?

What you need to establish is a regular regime or routine, where you pray at the same time and in the same place each day until it becomes a habit. Begin simply. Find a place that you can pray (not in bed!) that is quiet. Set a time, and go to that same place each day at the same time. This is your *date* with God. He will show up. You be faithful in this. Don't try to do too much. Don't set yourself up for failure by declaring. "I'm going to pray 2 hours a day, every day from now on." Be faithful in the *little* things. Don't despise *small* beginnings. If you are a neophyte pray-er, pray 15 minutes. With God quality really is better than quantity. The bottom line is to do it. Make up your mind that your prayer time is a priority. The rewards are great.

Paul's Prayers

How to Pray Effective Prayers and get your Prayers Answered!

Now you are ready to begin! Here are a few notes to help you negotiate through the rest of the book. God bless!

NOTES ON NEGOTIATING THE BOOK:

All of Paul's prayers (found in each of his letters) are transcribed on the following pages; However, this represents only a *partial list* of the prayers of confession. There are literally thousands of prayer confessions in the New Testament. While reading Paul's letters for yourself, you may be inspired to write many more.

A topical list of prayers (by subject) is listed at the back of this book, referenced by the letter-number combination found at the end of each prayer. The prayer categories are in bold. The letter is the name of the book; the number is the number of the prayer on the page. Example: C25 = the 5th prayer on the 2Corinthians page. G8 = 8th prayer on the Galatians page.

This is a working booklet. **Feel free to write in it**. Circle or highlight the prayers that really mean something to you. Make notes in the margins. Remember, because the Word is alive, different prayers will "jump out" or catch your attention at different times in your life. God will be speaking directly to you as you pray His Word given through Paul. *And my prayer for you is that God who can do immeasurably more than you can ask or even think, will keep you strong until the day that Christ appears, and that you will come to know Him even better.* [Eph 3:20]

Paul's Prayers
How to Pray Effective Prayers and get your Prayers Answered!

WORKBOOK

SECTION

Paul's Prayers

How to Pray Effective Prayers and get your Prayers Answered!

NOTES	PRAYERS	CONFESSIONS
	[Paul's Letter to the Romans]	*[Paul's Letter to the Romans]*

PRAYERS

[Paul's Letter to the Romans]

I pray that God our Father and our Lord Jesus Christ will be kind to you and will bless you with peace! *general* **R1**

I pray that God will make it possible for me to visit you. *[note: you can pray for personal, everyday things! He can make a way, when there seems to be no way.]* *opening doors* **R2**

I Pray that God, who rules over all, will be praised forever. Amen *encouragement, praise* **R3**

My greatest wish and prayer to God is for the people of Israel to be saved. I pray they would come to understand what makes them acceptable to God. *salvation* **R4**

I ask God to bless everyone who mistreats me, to bless and not to curse them. *forgiveness, hurt, enemies* **R5**

CONFESSIONS

[Paul's Letter to the Romans]

Thank You God, that by reading the Word, I do learn how God wants me to behave and I discover what is right. I am sure that you are my guide and my light when it is dark. *guidance, serving Him* **R6**

Than you God that I am acceptable to you because I have faith, even though I don't do *any*thing to deserve these blessings. Thank You God, that I can rest in this. *confidence, acceptance* **R7**

I think of myself as dead to the power of sin, but alive and living for God. Thank You God that by your Spirit, I will not let sin rule over my body. I will not obey it's desires or let any part of my body become a slave of evil. I give myself to God and am ruled by His kindness and not by the Law. *overcoming habits, drugs, overweight, sex sins, serving Him, consecration* **R8**

Paul's Prayers

How to Pray Effective Prayers and get your Prayers Answered!

NOTES	PRAYERS	CONFESSIONS
	[Paul's Letter to the Romans]	*[Paul's Letter to the Romans]*
	I pray that God who gives endurance and encouragement, will give you a spirit of unity among yourselves as you follow Christ Jesus *so that* with one heart and mouth you may glorify the God and Father of our Lord Jesus Christ. (We accept one another then, just as Christ has accepted us in order to bring praise to God) *consecration, patience, encouragement, unity, brotherly love, forgiveness* **R9**	I consider that my present sufferings are not worth comparing with the glory that will be revealed in me. *patience, strength* **R11**
	I pray that the God of hope will fill you with all joy and peace as you trust in Him, so that you may overflow with hope by the power of the Holy Spirit. *hope, faith* **R10**	Thank You God that Your Spirit helps me in my weakness. When I do not know what I ought to pray for, the Spirit himself intercedes for me with groans that Words cannot express. And God who searches my heart, knows the mind of the Spirit because the Spirit intercedes for me in accordance with God's will. *wisdom, understanding, insight, help, prayer* **R12**

Paul's Prayers

How to Pray Effective Prayers and get your Prayers Answered!

NOTES	PRAYERS	CONFESSIONS

[Paul's Letter to the Romans]

I pray that the grace of our Lord Jesus will be with you. *grace* **R13**

[Paul's Letter to the Romans]

I bless those who persecute me. I bless and do not curse. I will not repay anyone evil for evil, but will be careful to do what is right in the eyes of everybody, especially, you God. As far as it depends on me, I will live at peace with everyone. I will not take revenge, but leave room for God's wrath since vengeance is yours. *love, forgiveness* **R14**

I will not be overcome by evil, but will overcome evil with good. I will not take revenge, but leave room for God's wrath. *revenge, forgiveness, anger* **R15**

Paul's Prayers

How to Pray Effective Prayers and get your Prayers Answered!

YOUR NOTES / PRAYERS	CONFESSIONS
	[Paul's Letter to the Romans] I will submit myself to the governing authorities, for there is no authority accept that which God has established. ***obedience, submission* R16**
	I will behave decently, as in the daytime, not in orgies and drunkenness, not in sexual immorality and debauchery, not in dissension and jealousy. Rather, I clothe myself with the Lord Jesus Christ and do not <u>think</u> about how to gratify the desires of the sinful nature.. ***Overcoming habits, drugs, overweight, sex sins, anger, jealousy serving Him, consecration* R17**

Paul's Prayers

How to Pray Effective Prayers and get your Prayers Answered!

NOTES

PRAYERS
[Paul's First Letter to the Corinthians]

I pray grace and peace to you from God our Father and the Lord Jesus Christ. **grace, peace $C_1 1$**

I pray grace and peace to you from God our Father and the Lord Jesus Christ. **grace, peace $C_1 2$**

I would like (pray) every one of you to speak in tongues, but I would rather that you prophesy. He who prophesies is greater than one who speaks in tongues, unless he interprets, so that the church may be edified. **gifts of the spirit, tongues, prophesy $C_1 3$**

I pray that the grace of the Lord Jesus will be with you. **grace, peace $C_1 4$**

CONFESSIONS
[Paul's First Letter to the Corinthians]

My preaching was not with wise and persuasive words, but with a demonstration of the Spirit's power, so that your faith might not rest on men's wisdom, but on God's power. **preaching, teaching, signs and wonders, Holy Spirit $C_1 5$**

I speak words not taught by human wisdom, but in words taught by the Sprit, expressing spiritual truths in spiritual words **preaching, teaching, signs and wonders, Holy Spirit $C_1 6$**

The power of our Lord Jesus Christ is present when we are assembled in the name of our Lord Jesus. **Holy Spirit, power $C_1 7$**

Paul's Prayers

How to Pray Effective Prayers and get your Prayers Answered!

YOUR NOTES / PRAYERS	CONFESSIONS
	[Paul's First Letter to the Corinthians]
	All things come to me *from* God, the Father *for* whom I live; and *through* Jesus Christ *through* whom I live. **supply, answer prayer $C_1 8$**
	I thank You that You <u>do</u> supply my needs for those who preach the gospel should receive their living from the gospel. **supply, answer prayer $C_1 9$**
	I pray that I may interpret what I say, for if I pray in tongue, my spirit prays, but my mind is unfruitful and I would pray with my spirit, *and* my mind. **tongues, prophesy, gifts of the spirit $C_1 10$**

Paul's Prayers

How to Pray Effective Prayers and get your Prayers Answered!

YOUR NOTES / PRAYERS　　　**CONFESSIONS**

[Paul's First Letter to the Corinthians]

I pray that I will be on guard, standing firm in the faith --- that I will be courageous, strong, and do everything in love. **faith, love C₁11**

Paul's Prayers

How to Pray Effective Prayers and get your Prayers Answered!

NOTES	PRAYERS	CONFESSIONS

[Paul's Second Letter to the Corinthians]

I pray grace and peace to you from God our Father and the Lord Jesus Christ. **peace, grace $C_2 1$**

I pray to God that you will not do anything wrong. **life, sin $C_2 2$**

I pray that the grace of the Lord Jesus Christ and the love of God and the fellowship of the Holy Spirit be with you all. **peace, grace $C_2 3$**

I pray for your perfection. Aim for perfection, listen to my appeal (the word), be of one mind, live in peace, And the God of love and peace will be with you. **peace, grace, growth $C_2 4$**

[Paul's Second Letter to the Corinthians]

Thank You God that You, the Father of compassion and the God of all comfort, comforts me in all of my troubles so that I can comfort those in any trouble with the comfort that I myself have received from You. **comfort, trouble $C_2 5$**

Thank You Lord for opening doors for me. **guidance, help $C_2 6$**

Thank You God for removing the blinders before the mind's eyes of the unbelievers, so that they can see the light of the gospel of the glory of Christ, who is the image of God. **growth, glory, salvation $C_2 7$**

Paul's Prayers

How to Pray Effective Prayers and get your Prayers Answered!

YOUR NOTES / PRAYERS   CONFESSIONS

[Paul's Second Letter to the Corinthians]

Thank You God that you have given me the ministry of reconciliation– reconciling the world to yourself in Christ and that I am an ambassador for Christ as though You were making Your appeal to the world through me. **growth, glory, salvation C$_2$8**

Thank You God that I am a cheerful, prompt to do it giver and that you make all grace abound toward me so that I have all that I need and more than enough to do every good work and every charitable donation. **giving C$_2$9**

Paul's Prayers

How to Pray Effective Prayers and get your Prayers Answered!

YOUR NOTES / PRAYERS **CONFESSIONS**

[Paul's Second Letter to the Corinthians]

May You who have supplied seed for sowing and bread for food (God) also supply and increase my store of seed and increase the harvest of my righteousness. **giving C$_2$10**

Thank You God for enriching me in every way so that I can be generous on every occasion, so that my generosity will result in thanksgiving to You. **giving C$_2$11**

Paul's Prayers

How to Pray Effective Prayers and get your Prayers Answered!

NOTES	PRAYERS	CONFESSIONS

[Paul's Letter to the Galatians]

Grace and peace to you from God our Father and the Lord Jesus Christ who gave himself for our sins to rescue us from the present evil age, according to the will of our God and Father – to whom be glory for ever and ever. **grace, peace, freedom, sin G1**

I pray that the grace of the Lord Jesus will be with you. **grace, peace G2**

Peace and mercy to all who follow this rule (neither circumcision nor uncircumcision mean anything, what counts is a new creation). **peace, mercy, law G3**

I pray that the grace of the Lord Jesus will be with your spirit. **grace, peace G4**

[Paul's Letter to the Galatians]

Thank You God for giving me your Spirit to work miracles. **miracles, signs and wonders, Spirit G5**

Thank You God that I am not alienated from Christ nor have I fallen away from grace, for by grace am I saved and delivered (from all my circumstances). **grace, deliverance, salvation G6**

I thank you God that I owe no man but to love him. **debt, love G7**

Thank You God that I live by the Spirit and so do not gratify the desires of my sinful nature. **sin, overcoming habits G8**

Paul's Prayers

How to Pray Effective Prayers and get your Prayers Answered!

YOUR NOTES / PRAYERS	CONFESSIONS
	[Paul's Letter to the Galatians]
	Thank You God for wisdom. I am not deceived. You are not mocked. What a man sows, he reaps. Thank You that I do not sow to please my sinful nature and so reap destruction, but I sow to please the Spirit and from the Spirit reap eternal life. **sin, reap and sow G9**
	I do not become weary in well doing, for I know that in the proper time, I will reap a harvest if I do not give up. **blessing, good deeds, rewards G10**

Paul's Prayers

How to Pray Effective Prayers and get your Prayers Answered!

NOTES	PRAYERS	CONFESSIONS
	[Paul's Letter to the Ephesians]	*[Paul's Letter to the Ephesians]*

<table>
<tr><td></td><td>

Grace and peace to you from God our Father and the Lord Jesus Christ. **grace, peace, E1**

I keep asking (praying) that the God of our Lord Jesus Christ, the glorious Father, may give you the Spirit of wisdom and revelation, *so that* you may <u>know</u> him better. **wisdom, revelation, insight E2**

I pray also that the eyes of your heart may be enlightened in order that you may know the hope to which He has called you, the riches of His glorious inheritance in the saints, and His incomparably great power for us who believe. **insight, wisdom, calling, power E3**

</td><td>

thank you God that You work out everything in conformity with the purpose of Your will. I can relax in You. **comfort, guidance, peace E6**

Thank You God, that because of Your great love for me, you, who are rich in mercy, made me alive with Christ — even when I was dead in my transgressions. It is by grace that I have been saved (delivered), and it is by grace that I will continue to be saved and delivered from my present circumstances. **deliverance, mercy, grace E7**

</td></tr>
</table>

Paul's Prayers

How to Pray Effective Prayers and get your Prayers Answered!

NOTES	PRAYERS	CONFESSIONS
		[Paul's Letter to the Ephesians]
	[Paul's Letter to the Ephesians]	God, show me what You would have me do. You said that I was Your workmanship, created in Christ Jesus to do good works, which You prepared in advance for me to do. Show me the good works. **guidance, dedication, submission E8**
	I pray that out of His glorious riches, He may strengthen you with power through His Spirit in your inner being, *so that* Christ may dwell in your hearts through faith. **strength, power E4**	
	And I pray that you, being rooted and established in love, may have power, together with all the saints, to grasp how wide and long and high and deep is the love of Christ, and to *KNOW* this love that surpasses knowledge – that you may be filled to the measure of all the fullness of God. **love, power E5**	Thank You, God, that I can approach you with freedom and confidence because I am in Christ Jesus and have faith in Him. **comfort, peace, prayer E9**
		I will live a life worthy of the calling to which You have called me -- that I would be completely humble and gentle; patient, bearing with one another in love. **guidance, submission E10**

Paul's Prayers
How to Pray Effective Prayers and get your Prayers Answered!

NOTES	PRAYERS	CONFESSIONS

[Paul's Letter to the Ephesians]

[Paul's Letter to the Ephesians]

Now to Him who is able to do immeasurably more than all we ask or imagine, according to His power that is at work within us, to Him be glory in the church and in Christ Jesus throughout all generations, for ever and ever! Amen. **general, answer E10**

I pray that whenever I open my mouth, Words may be given me so that I will fearlessly make known the mystery of the gospel – that I would declare it fearlessly as I should. **boldness, fear, preaching E11**

I will make every effort to keep the unity of the Spirit through the bond of peace. **consecration, patience, love E14**

I will put off my old self, with regard to my former way of life, which is being corrupted by its deceitful desires; and be made new in the attitude of my mind. I put on my new self, created to be like God in true righteousness and holiness. **consecration, holiness, overcoming habits E15**

I will be strong in the Lord and in His mighty power, putting on the whole armor of God so that I can take my stand against the devil's schemes. **power E16**

Paul's Prayers

How to Pray Effective Prayers and get your Prayers Answered!

NOTES	PRAYERS	CONFESSIONS
	[Paul's Letter to the Ephesians]	
	Peace to the brothers, and love with faith from God the Father and the Lord Jesus Christ. **love, faith, peace E12**	
	Grace to all who love our Lord Jesus with an undying love. **grace E13**	

Paul's Prayers

How to Pray Effective Prayers and get your Prayers Answered!

NOTES   **PRAYERS**   **CONFESSIONS**

[Paul's Letter to the Philippians]

Grace and peace to you from God our Father and the Lord Jesus Christ. **grace, peace P1**

And this is my prayer: That your love may abound more and more in knowledge and depth of insight, so that you may be able to discern what is best and may be pure and blameless until the day of Christ, filled with the fruit of righteousness that comes through Jesus Christ – to the glory and praise of God. **love, insight P2**

And my God will meet all your needs according to His glorious riches in Christ Jesus. **supply, needs P3**

[Paul's Letter to the Philippians]

I thank God that He who began a good work in me will carry it on to completion until the day of Christ Jesus. **consecration, Guidance, peace P4**

I thank God that I stand firm in one spirit, contending as one man for the faith of the gospel, without being frightened in any way by those who oppose me. This is a sign to them that they will be destroyed, but a sign to me that I will be saved – and that by God. **deliverance, peace P5**

Paul's Prayers

How to Pray Effective Prayers and get your Prayers Answered!

NOTES	PRAYERS	CONFESSIONS
		[Paul's Letter to the Philippians]
		I know that through your prayers and the help given by the Spirit of Jesus Christ, that what has happened to me will turn out for my deliverance. I eagerly expect and hope that I will in no way be ashamed. **deliverance, consecration, holiness P8**
	[Paul's Letter to the Philippians]	
	To our God and Father, be glory for ever and ever. Amen. **glory P6**	
		I pray that we will be like-minded, having the same love, being one in spirit and purpose – not looking only to our own interests, but also to those of others. **love, generosity P9**
	The grace of the Lord Jesus Christ be with your spirit. Amen. **grace P7**	
		God works in me to will and to do (act) according to His good purpose. **guidance, dedication P10**

-36-

Paul's Prayers
How to Pray Effective Prayers and get your Prayers Answered!

NOTES	PRAYERS	CONFESSIONS
		[Paul's Letter to the Philippians] I consider everything a loss compared to the surpassing greatness of knowing Christ Jesus my Lord-- that I may gain Christ and be found in him, not having a righteousness of my own, but that which is through faith in Christ. **righteousness, eternal life, knowledge P11** But one thing I do: Forgetting what is behind and straining toward what is ahead, I press on toward the goal to win the prize for which God has called me heavenward in Christ Jesus. **dedication, serving Him P12**

Paul's Prayers

How to Pray Effective Prayers and get your Prayers Answered!

NOTES	PRAYERS	CONFESSIONS
		[Paul's Letter to the Philippians]
		I am not anxious for anything, but in all things by prayer and petition with thanksgiving, I make my request known to God. And the peace of God which surpasses all understanding guards my heart and mind in Christ Jesus. **prayer, peace P13**
		I can do anything through Christ who gives me strength. **dedication, strength, power P14**

Paul's Prayers

How to Pray Effective Prayers and get your Prayers Answered!

NOTES	PRAYERS	CONFESSIONS

[Paul's Letter to the Colossians]

I pray that God our Father will be kind to you and will bless you with peace! **peace Co1**

We have not stopped praying for you since the first we heard about you. In fact, we always pray that God will show you everything He wants you to do and that you may have all the wisdom and understanding that His Spirit gives. Then, you will live a life that honors the Lord, and you will always please Him by doing good deeds. You will come to know God even better. His glorious power will make you patient and strong enough to endure anything, and you will be truly happy. **guidance, dedication, wisdom Co2**

[Paul's Letter to the Colossians]

I tell others about You in demonstration of power and not in mere words. You give me the wisdom and the Words to speak as you'd have me speak in order to convince people and family to turn and to rely on You -- and You alone. **guidance, dedication, wisdom Co3**

I thank you God that the forces of the universe don't have any power over me. **power Co4**

-39-

Paul's Prayers

How to Pray Effective Prayers and get your Prayers Answered!

NOTES	Prayers	CONFESSIONS

[Paul's Letter to the Colossians]

I pray that you will be grateful to God for letting you have part in what He has promised His people in the kingdom of light. **guidance, dedication, wisdom Co5**

I pray that God will be kind to you. **grace, mercy Co6**

[Paul's Letter to the Colossians]

God, keep me from the appearance of loving You without the depth of feeling; keep me from hypocrisy. Show me Lord, what You would have me do. Help me Lord to be true to You, and not to religion. My allegiance belongs to You. **guidance, dedication, wisdom Co7**

My mind is on things above, and I am becoming more and more like You, knowing You better. **guidance, dedicationCo8**

Thank You that I have given up my old way of life with its habits; I am a new, overcoming person in You. **guidance, dedication, overcoming habits Co9**

Paul's Prayers

How to Pray Effective Prayers and get your Prayers Answered!

YOUR NOTES / PRAYERS **CONFESSIONS**

[Paul's Letter to the Colossians]

Whatever I do or say, I do in the name of the Lord Jesus, as I give thanks to God the Father because of Him. **thankfulness, dedication Co10**

God makes a way for me to spread His message and explain the mystery about Christ. **salvation, eternal life Co11**

Paul's Prayers

How to Pray Effective Prayers and get your Prayers Answered!

NOTES	PRAYERS	CONFESSIONS

[Paul's First Letter to the Thessalonians]

I Pray that God will be kind to you and will bless you with peace. **mercy, grace Th$_1$1**

We always thank God that you believed the message that we preached. You accepted it as God's message and now it is working in you. **obedience, guidance Th$_1$2**

We pray that God our Father and our Lord Jesus will let us visit you. **direction, guidance Th$_1$3**

May the Lord make your love for each other and for everyone else grow by leaps and bounds. **love Th$_1$4**

[Paul's First Letter to the Thessalonians]

God don't let me be deceived into thinking I'm OK When I'm not-- thinking I am safe and secure when destruction is at hand. Father God, help me not to live in darkness. I belong to the light, help me to live in the day. Help me to stay awake and be alert, especially as the judgment day approaches. Help me to stay sober and let my faith and love be like a suit of armor. **help, deliverance, faithfulness Th$_1$5**

Father God, don't let me be hateful to others because they are hateful to me. Rather, let me be good to others and overcome evil with good. **love, forgiveness Th$_1$6**

Paul's Prayers

How to Pray Effective Prayers and get your Prayers Answered!

NOTES	PRAYERS	CONFESSIONS

[Paul's First Letter to the Thessalonians]

I pray that He will make your hearts pure and innocent in the sight of God the Father. **holiness, righteousness, dedication Th$_1$7**

I pray that God, who gives peace, will make you completely holy. And may your spirit, soul, and body be kept healthy and faultless until our Lord Jesus Christ returns. **holiness, peace, healing Th$_1$8**

I pray that our Lord Jesus Christ will be kind to you **mercy, grace Th$_1$9**

[Paul's First Letter to the Thessalonians]

Holy Spirit, I welcome You. Speak to and through me. You are welcome in this place. **holiness, faithfulness Th$_1$10**

Paul's Prayers

How to Pray Effective Prayers and get your Prayers Answered!

NOTES | PRAYERS | CONFESSIONS

[Paul's Second Letter to the Thessalonians]

[Paul's Second Letter to the Thessalonians]

I pray that God our Father and the Lord Jesus Christ will be kind to you and will bless you with peace! **mercy, grace Th₂1**

Although I am having trouble and suffering, I do not let go of my faith. I continue in patience, waiting for Your promised deliverance. **suffering, tribulation, deliverance Th₂3**

We keep praying that God will make you worthy of being His people. We pray for God's power to help you do all the good things that you hope to do and that your faith makes you want to do. Because God and our Lord Jesus Christ are so kind, you will bring honor to the name of our Lord Jesus, and He will bring honor to you. **righteousness, dedication Th₂2**

Father God, don't let me be deceived into loving to do evil rather than believing the truth. Don't allow me to be fooled into believing a lie. Help me to love the truth and accept it! **faith, faithfulness, sin Th₂4**

Keep me safe from worthless and evil people. I know that You Lord can be trusted to make me strong and protect me from harm. **deliverance, protection Th₂5**

Paul's Prayers

How to Pray Effective Prayers and get your Prayers Answered!

| NOTES | PRAYERS | CONFESSIONS |

[Paul's Second Letter to the Thessalonians]

We pray that our Lord Jesus Christ and God our Father will encourage you and help you always to do and say the right things. **dedication, faithfulness, sin Th₂6**

I pray that the Lord will guide you to be as loving as God and as patient as Christ. **love, patience Th₂7**

I pray that the Lord, who gives peace, will always bless you with peace. May the Lord be with all of you. **peace Th₂8**

I pray that our Lord Jesus Christ will be kind to all of you. **Mercy, grace Th₂9**

Paul's Prayers

How to Pray Effective Prayers and get your Prayers Answered!

NOTES	PRAYERS	CONFESSIONS

[Paul's First Letter to Timothy]

[Paul's First Letter to Timothy]

I pray that God our Father and our Lord Jesus Christ will be kind and merciful to you. May they bless you with peace! **Mercy, Grace $T_1 1$**

Thank You God for the wisdom to have genuine love, as well as a good conscience and true faith. I will not give these up for empty talk. Help me to see the truth and to see it clearly – to walk in Your ways and no one else's. **consecration, faithfulness $T_1 4$**

I thank Christ Jesus our Lord who has given me the strength for my work because He knew that He could trust me. **Faithfulness, Strength $T_1 2$**

I will always listen to my conscience and in so doing, not make a mess of my faith. **faith, faithfulness $T_1 5$**

I pray that honor and glory will always be given to the only God who lives forever and is the invisible and eternal King! Amen. **Honor, Glory $T_1 3$**

God, help and bless my family. I thank You for each one of them. **love, blessings $T_1 6$**

Paul's Prayers

How to Pray Effective Prayers and get your Prayers Answered!

NOTES	PRAYERS	CONFESSIONS

[Paul's First Letter to Timothy]

Slight difference: Paul's instructions for your prayers
First of all, I ask you to pray for everyone. Ask God to help and bless them all, and tell God how thankful you are for each of them. Pray for kings and others in power, so that we may live quiet and peaceful lives as we worship and honor God. **Authority, peace T₁7**

I pray that the Lord will be kind to all of you! **peace T₁8**

[Paul's First Letter to Timothy]

I pray for the President, my boss, my Pastor, and all those in authority over me. I ask that You guide them in wisdom and give them peace; so that I may live a quiet, peaceable life in all godliness as I worship and honor You. **authority, peace T₁9**

I will be self-controlled, sensible, well-behaved, friendly and able to teach. I will remain sober, not being a heavy drinker or a troublemaker, but instead I'll be kind and gentle. Keep me, Lord from being a lover of money. **control, overcoming habits T₁10**

Paul's Prayers
How to Pray Effective Prayers and get your Prayers Answered!

YOUR NOTES / PRAYERS	CONFESSIONS
	[Paul's First Letter to Timothy]
	My children will be obedient and I will keep my household in order. **obedience $T_1 11$**
	I will not be one of those who turn from the faith and are fooled by evil spirits and by teachings that come from demons; instead I will continually listen to You, being quick to hear and obey Your commandments and teachings. **consecration, faithfulness, insight $T_1 12$**

Paul's Prayers

How to Pray Effective Prayers and get your Prayers Answered!

YOUR NOTES / PRAYERS	CONFESSIONS
	[Paul's First Letter to Timothy] I will set an example for others to follow by what I say and do, as well as by my love, faith, and purity. By doing this, I will not only save myself, but the people who hear and see me. **faithfulness, love, witness $T_1 13$**
	I will show my Christian faith by the care I give to my relatives and especially my family. **love, obedience $T_1 14$**
	I will not fall prey to the love of money and become corrupt, being led astray and falling into all kinds of grief. Instead, I put my trust in You Lord who richly provides, even for my enjoyment. **needs, supply, power $T_1 15$**

Paul's Prayers

get your Prayers Answered!

CONFESSIONS

Father and our Lord Christ Jesus will be kind and merciful to you and will bless you with peace. **peace, mercy T₂1**

I pray that the Lord will be kind to the family of Onesiphorus. He often cheered me up and wasn't ashamed of me when I was put in jail... I pray that the Lord Jesus will ask God to show mercy to Onesiphorus on the day of judgment. *[definitely pray a blessing for those people who have blessed and helped you – even praying for their families! Make their way smoother through your prayers.]* **love, blessings T₂2**

me the promise that Christ makes possible. **consecration, salvation T₂3**

Thank You Lord for giving me power, love, and self-control. I am not ashamed to speak for You, and will use your power to speak your good news -- the gospel of Christ -- in my environment. **fear preaching, serving Him T₂4**

God, bless _____ and his family. Have mercy on them and be kind to them because they have helped me by _____. **love, blessings T₂5**

Paul's Prayers

How to Pray Effective Prayers and get your Prayers Answered!

NOTES	PRAYERS	CONFESSIONS

[Paul's Second Letter to Timothy]

[Paul's Second Letter to Timothy]

I pray that the Lord will bless your life and will be kind to you. **mercy, blessings T$_2$6**

I determine to stop doing evil and through Your Spirit will make myself pure, so that I will become special – that my life will be holy and pleasing to You, and I'll be able to do all kinds of good deeds. . **overcoming habits, consecration, holiness, serving Him T$_2$7**

Lord, keep me from being harmed by evil, and bring me safely into Your heavenly kingdom. **salvation, suffering, trouble T$_2$8**

[Paul's Letter to Titus] *[Paul's Letter to Titus]*

I pray that God our Father and Christ Jesus our Savior will be kind to you and will bless you with peace! **peace, mercy Ti1**

I pray that I will have more faith and be able to understand the truth about religion, so that I will have the hope of eternal life that God promised long ago. **insight, eternal life Ti3**

I pray that the Lord will be kind to all of you! **mercy Ti2**

Paul's Prayers

How to Pray Effective Prayers and get your Prayers Answered!

NOTES   PRAYERS

[Paul's Letter to Philemon]

Grace to you and peace from God our Father and the Lord Jesus Christ. **peace, grace Pi1**

I always thank my God as I remember you in my prayers, because I hear about your faith in the Lord Jesus and your love for all the saints. I pray that you may be active in sharing your faith, so that you will have a full understanding of every good thing we have in Christ. **faith, love, wisdom Pi2**

I pray that our Lord Jesus Christ will be kind to you **mercy, grace Pi3**

Anger, R15, R17
Answer, $C_1$8, $C_1$9, E10
Authority, $T_1$4, $T_1$9
Blessings, G10, $T_1$8, $T_2$2, $T_2$3, $T_2$6
Boldness, E11
Brotherly love, R10,
Calling, E3,
Comfort, $C_2$5, E6, E9
Confidence, R7
Consecration, R8, R10, R17, E14, E15, P6, P8, $T_1$6, $T_1$12, $T_2$4, $T_2$7
Control, $T_1$10
Debt, G7
Dedication, E8, P10, P12, P14, Co2, Co3, Co5, Co7, Co8, Co9, Co10, $Th_1$5, $Th_2$2, $Th_2$3
Deliverance, G6, E7, P7, P8, Th18, Th27, Th29

Drugs, R8, R17
Encouragement, R3, R10
Enemies, R5
Eternal life, P11, Co11, Ti3
Faith, R11, $C_1$11, E12, $Th_2$8, $T_1$7, Pi2
Faithfulness, $Th_1$8, $Th_1$10, $Th_2$3, $Th_2$8, $T_1$2, $T_1$6, $T_1$7, $T_1$12, $T_1$13
Fear, E11, $T_2$5
Forgiveness, R5, R10, R14, R15, Th19
Freedom, G1
General, R1, E10
Generosity, P9
Gifts of the Spirit, C13, C110
Giving, C29, C210, C211
Glory, C27, C28, P4, T13
Good deeds, G10

$C_2$1, $C_2$3, $C_2$4, G1, G2, G4, G6, E1, E7, E13, P1, P5, Co4, $Th_1$1, $Th_1$7, $Th_2$1, $Th_2$6, $T_1$1, Pi1, Pi3
Growth, $C_2$4, $C_2$7, $C_2$8,
Guidance, R6, $C_2$6, E6, E8, P6, P10, Co2, C03, Co5, Co7, Co8, Co9, $Th_1$2, $Th_1$3
Healing, $Th_1$6 8
Help, R13, $C_2$6, $Th_1$8
Holiness, E15, P8, $Th_1$5, $Th_1$6, $Th_1$10, $T_2$7
Holy Spirit, $C_1$5, $C_1$6, $C_1$7
Honor, $T_1$3
Hope, R11,
Hurt, R5
Insight, R13, E2, P2, T112, Ti3
Jealousy, R17
Knowledge, P11

Paul's Prayers: Topical Index

Bible Book Abbreviations

R – Romans
C_1 – 1st Corinthians
C_2 – 2nd Corinthians
G – Galatians

E – Ephesians
P – Philippians
Co – Colossians
Th_1 – 1st Thessalonians
Th_2 – 2nd Thessalonians

T1 – 1st Timothy
T_2 – 2nd Timothy
Ti – Titus
Ph – Philemon

Law, G3
Life, $C_2$2
Love, R14, $C_1$11, G7, E5, E14, E12, P2, P9, $Th_1$4, $Th_1$9, $Th_2$4, $T_1$8, $T_1$13, $T_1$14, $T_2$2, $T_2$6, Pi2
Mercy, G3, E7, Co4, $Th_1$1, $Th_1$7, $Th_2$1, $Th_2$6, $T_1$1, $T_2$1, $T_2$3, Ti1, Ti2, Pi3
Miracles, G5
Needs, P3, $T_1$15
Obedience, R16, $Th_1$2, $T_1$11, $T_1$14
Opening doors, R2
Overcoming habits, R8, R17, G8, E15, Co9, $T_1$10, $T_2$7
Overweight, R8, R17
Patience, R9, R10, E14, Th24

Peace, C11, C12, C14, C21, C23, C24, G1, G2, G3, G4, E1, E6, E9, E12, P1, P6, P7, P13, Co1, $Th_1$6, Th25, T14, T15, T19, T21, Ti1, Pi1
Power, C17, E3, E4, E16, P14, Co6, T115
Praise, R3,
Prayer, R13, E9, P13
Preaching, $C_1$5, $C_1$6, E11, $T_2$5
Prophecy, $C_1$3, $C_1$10
Protection, $Th_2$9
Reap and sow, G9
Revelation, E2
Revenge, R15
Rewards, G10
Righteousness, P11, $Th_1$5, $Th_2$2
Salvation, R4, C27, C28, G6, Co11, T24, T28

Serving Him, R6, R8, R17, P12, $T_2$5, $T_2$7
Sex sins, R8, R17
Signs and wonders, $C_1$5, $C_1$6, G5,
Sin, $C_2$2, G1, G8, G9, $Th_2$3, $Th_2$8
Spirit, G5,
Strength, R9, E4, E5, P14, $T_1$2
Submission, E8, R16
Suffering, $Th_2$7, $T_2$8
Supply, $C_1$8, $C_1$9, P3, $T_1$15
Teaching, $C_1$5, C16
Thankfulness, Co10
Tongues, $C_1$3, $C_1$10
Tribulation, $Th_2$7
Trouble, $C_2$5, $T_2$8
Understanding, R13
Unity, R10,
Wisdom, R13, E2, E3, Co2, Co3, Co5, Co7, Pi2
Witness, $T_1$13

Printed in the United States
35231LVS00005B/298-534